SKUNKS
AFTER DARK

Heather M. Moore Niver

Enslow Publishing
101 W. 23rd Street
Suite 240
New York, NY 10011
USA

enslow.com

Words to Know

gland—An organ in an animal's body that makes and gets rid of a product.

grasslands—Large open areas of land that are covered with grass.

habitat— The place in which an animal lives.

mammals—Animals that have a backbone and hair, usually give birth to live babies, and produce milk to feed their young.

omnivores—Animals that eat both plants and animals.

predators—Animals that kill and eat other animals to stay alive.

prowling—Moving about quietly and secretly.

Contents

Shy Skunk

On a quiet night in the woods, a skunk is **prowling** for food. But suddenly it hears something in the trees. A curious coyote starts forward, but stops and sniffs. The skunk begins to stomp its feet. The coyote pauses. It is hungry. The coyote starts forward. This is too close for the skunk. It turns to leave and raises its fluffy black-and-white tail. It sprays a stinky liquid right into the coyote's eyes. The coyote yelps as its eyes begin to sting. The skunk ambles into the woods, safe from the jaws of a coyote once again.

FUN FACT!

Skunks are **omnivores**. Plants, fruit, eggs, or insects will do. Even a small **mammal** or other tiny animal would be a good meal.

Skunks will eat just about anything they can find. This striped skunk is eating a wasp's nest.

Hello, Skunks

Have you seen a skunk? If not, you have probably at least smelled one! Skunks are black-and-white mammals. They are well known for their smell. There are eleven different species, or kinds, of skunks. Nine kinds of skunks live across North and South America.

Two kinds of skunks live in Asia. These are the Malayan stink badger and the Palawan stink badger. Stink badgers used to be thought of as badgers. In 1990 scientists realized they were closer relatives to skunks!

FUN FACT!

Skunks are sometimes known as polecats in the United States. Their name comes from the Latin language. It means "bad odor."

Skunks are easy to recognize by their black-and-white fur.

All skunks are black and white. Their patterns are different though. The common striped skunk has mostly black fur. Its white stripe is in a V shape down its back. Common striped skunks also have a white bar between their eyes. Other skunks might have stripes, spots, or even swirls. These striking patterns make skunks very easy to spot.

Skunks are all different sizes. Most skunks are about the size of a housecat. Most are from 8 to 19 inches (20 to 48 centimeters). Their tails add another 5 to 15 inches (13 to 38 cm).

FUN FACT!

Skunks have a great sense of smell. They use their noses to find food. But their eyesight is quite poor.

The common skunk has a V-shaped white stripe on its back.

Oh, Stink!

You can see that black-and-white pattern from far away. That's a good thing! Once you get a whiff, you'll understand why. Skunks know how to put up a stink!

Most of the time, skunks are quiet and calm. When a skunk is threatened, it has a few ways to scare off the **predator**. Some species stamp their feet to show anger. Sometimes they make noise, hissing and snarling. Some skunks even do a handstand. They move toward the threat. If these things don't work, the skunk has another trick under its tail!

This spotted skunk is calm, but if it feels threatened, it will do a handstand to scare off a predator.

A skunk has two **glands**. They are at the back of the body, under the tail. These glands contain a stinky, oily liquid. If a skunk can't scare off a predator, it arches its back and turns around. Then it raises its tail and sprays. The spray can cause blindness and lots of pain if it reaches the predator's eyes. Blindness does not last very long. The spray can cause headaches and vomiting. Usually, the spray is just uncomfortable and annoying. The oily liquid is very difficult to remove.

FUN FACT!

Striped and hooded skunks will sometimes charge at a predator. When they are mad, they spray. They can face their head at the predator as they spray.

If it can't scare off a predator, a skunk sprays a bad-smelling liquid.

A skunk's spray can reach 12 feet (3.7 meters)! They have muscles that allow them to control the spray. They can aim very well up to 6 feet (1.8 m). They often aim for the face if they can.

But what does a skunk do if it is being chased? Stopping would be dangerous! It has another stinky trick. As it is running away, it cannot see where the predator is. So the skunk sprays a cloud of bad-smelling mist. The predator has to run through the funky fog if it wants to keep chasing the skunk.

FUN FACT!

A stink badger will pretend to be dead if it can't escape. It "dies" with its glands facing the predator. When the threat gets close enough, it sprays!

A skunk raises its tail as it gets ready to spray its enemy.

Home, Sweet-Smelling Home

For such a smelly beast, you might think that skunks also have messy homes. They do not! Skunks like a comfortable den. Often they bring in leaves and grass to make it warm and cozy.

Skunks may spend their days in hollowed logs or piles of brush. They may also enjoy burrows made by another animal. Sometimes they hang out under buildings or even in walls. They might dig their own dens, too.

Skunks like to travel. They often only spend a few months at a time in a den.

FUN FACT!

Skunks live in all kinds of **habitats**. They live in deserts, **grasslands**, forests, and mountains. Some even live in cities.

Skunks prefer to keep their dens clean and comfy.

Skunks usually like to live on their own. Sometimes when the weather is very cold, females will share a den together. Their bodies keep each other from being too cold.

Males and females will come together to start a family. But it's a short meeting. After mating, the female chases off the male. Sometimes a male tries to get too friendly with a female who is not ready to mate. To discourage the male, the female sprays him. That's a clear sign she is not in the mood for romance!

Most of the time, skunks are solitary creatures.

So Stinkin' Cute!

Mother skunks usually give birth in the spring. Most skunks raise their babies all on their own. Baby skunks are called kittens, or kits. They usually have two to twelve kits between late April and early June.

Baby skunks are born blind. Their eyes don't open for a few weeks after birth. They are also born toothless.

But don't think that just because they're small their stink can't pack a punch. These little stinkers can spray before their eyes open!

FUN FACT!

Striped, hog-nosed, and hooded skunks start their families in February or March. The western spotted skunk waits until autumn.

Baby skunks are cute, but don't get too close! They can spray.

Spotted, Small, and Super Stinky

Spotted skunks are one of the smallest members of the skunk family. They are about the same size as a squirrel. It can follow animals like rodents into tighter spaces. Other skunks are too big to squeeze through small holes.

There are two kinds of spotted skunks. Eastern spotted skunks are a little bigger than western. Spotted skunks are also very stinky! They are well known as being much smellier than their striped skunk relatives. Spotted skunks are fast, too. They are excellent climbers. Spotted skunks are rarely seen. They almost never go out during the daytime.

FUN FACT!

The pygmy spotted skunk might be the smallest skunk. They can be as small as 4.5 inches (11.5 cm). One could fit in your hand!

The spotted skunk is one of the most creative sprayers in the skunk family! They are also very good at climbing trees.

Safety Stripes

Most predators don't bother skunks. If they are very hungry, large birds like eagles will attack skunks though. Some scientists think this is because birds have a poor sense of smell.

Recently scientists discovered something unusual about skunks. They think that the bold black-and-white color helps keep skunks safe. That pattern warns would-be predators. It communicates that this animal will put up a big stink if bothered. Sometimes the white stripes work as arrows. They point to the scent glands. Swirls and spots might help those skunks hide better.

FUN FACT!

Skunks are cute and do look a lot like cats. It might seem like a fun idea to bring one home. But in some states, it is illegal to keep a wild animal as a pet. Be sure and check local laws.

Skunks are designed to stick out. From their smell to their bold black-and-white fur, skunks warn predators to leave them alone!

Skunk Life

Skunks don't live very long in the wild. Most of the time, they live to be only about three years old. Sometimes a hard winter will kill weaker skunks. Other times, cars are to blame. Remember, skunks don't have very good eyesight. They follow their noses. Sometimes they end up looking for food in the road. Sometimes they stop in the street to eat. Then they can get hit by a car. Skunks live longer in protected areas, such as zoos.

Sometimes skunks wander into the road for food.

Sometimes skunks are hunted. They are desired for their funky patterned fur. People especially like their black-and-white stripes. Sometimes they are killed because people think they are pests. In some areas, humans eat them.

But skunks are good animals to have around. Part of their diet is made up of insects. These same bugs would ruin crops that we need for food. They also eat small mammals like rats or mice that can cause problems in barns. Spotted skunks are known to be extra good hunters. They are fast!

Although skunks hunt and eat insects and small mammals, they sometimes also eat bird eggs. This nest of turkey eggs will be a striped skunk's next meal.

Stay Safe
Around Skunks

Usually, skunks are shy. They like to keep away from you as much as you want to keep away from them! But if they are surprised, they'll let you know. Here are some ways to stay safe around skunks:

 Skunks have poor eyesight. Sometimes they fall into wells or holes. Place a board into the hole to help it escape. They are not great climbers, so make sure the board is not at a steep angle.

 Skunks follow their noses for food. They may wander into your garage or other building. Make sure the door is open at dusk. Close it after dark. Leave a line of flour to cause the skunk to leave white footprints. Then you can be sure it's out.

 Remove any seeds, birdseed, or similar tasty treats or seal them in containers.

 Sometimes skunks look for food during the day. If it seems to be looking for food, leave it alone.

 You may see a skunk walk in circles, seem to be lame, attack without warning, or not seem to be afraid at all. Call a wildlife specialist if you see a skunk acting like this.

 If you or a pet gets "skunked," you need to get rid of that stink! A bath in tomato juice with vinegar might help the smell. Other recipes include peroxide, and there are cleaners you can buy to get the oil out.

Learn More

Books

Gish, Melissa. *Living Wild: Skunks*. Mankato, MN: Creative Education, 2014.

Lockwood, Sophie. *Skunks*. Mankato, MN.: Child's World, 2014. Kindle ed.

Shoemaker, Karen. *Skunk Stench*. New York: Gareth Stevens Publishing, 2014.

Taylor, Barbara. *Stinky Skunks and Other Animal Adaptations*. New York: Crabtree Publishing Company, 2014.

Websites

A–Z Animals
a-z-animals.com/animals/skunk
Maps and photos help readers learn more about skunks.

National Geographic Kids
kids.nationalgeographic.com/animals/skunk/#skunk-babies-walking.jpg
Check out photos, facts, maps, and more!

Pittsburgh Zoo
pittsburghzoo.org/animal.aspx?id=73
This site features photos and facts about striped skunks.

Index

To Abbey, who has always known: Skunks don't smell bad, they just smell too much!

Published in 2016 by Enslow Publishing, LLC.
101 W. 23rd Street, Suite 240, New York, NY 10011

Copyright © 2016 by Enslow Publishing, LLC.

All rights reserved.

No part of this book may be reproduced by any means without the written permission of the publisher.

Library of Congress Cataloging-in-Publication Data

Niver, Heather M. Moore.
Skunks after dark / by Heather M. Moore Niver.
p. cm. — (Animals of the night)
Includes bibliographical references and index.
ISBN 978-0-7660-7360-9 (library binding)
ISBN 978-0-7660-7358-6 (pbk.)
ISBN 978-0-7660-7359-3 (6-pack)
1. Skunks — Juvenile literature. 2. Nocturnal animals — Juvenile literature. I. Niver, Heather Moore. II. Title.
QL737.C248 N58 2015
599.76'8—d23

Printed in the United States of America

To Our Readers: We have done our best to make sure all website addresses in this book were active and appropriate when we went to press. However, the author and the publisher have no control over and assume no liability for the material available on those websites or on any websites they may link to. Any comments or suggestions can be sent by e-mail to customerservice@enslow.com.

Photo Credits: Throughout book, narvikk/E+/Getty Images (starry background), kimberrywood/Digital Vision Vectors/Getty Images (green moon dingbat); cover, p. 1 Eric Isselee/Shutterstock.com (skunk), samxmed/E+/Getty Images (moon); p. 3 Eric Isselee/Shutterstock.com; p. 5 S.J. Krasemann/Photolibrary/Getty Images; p. 7 Heiko Kiera/Shutterstock.com; p. 9 Howard Sokol/Photolibrary/Getty Images; p. 11 Juniors/Juniors/SuperStock; p. 13 Holly Kuchera/iStock/Thinkstock; p. 15 © Leszczynski, Zigmund/Animals Animals—Earth Scenes; p. 17 Wayne Lynch/All Canada Photos/Getty Images; p. 19 Comstock Images/Stockbyte/Thinkstock; p. 21 Critterbiz/Shutterstock.com; p. 23 Jared Hobbs/All Canada Photos/Getty Images; p. 25 Tome Brakefield/Stockbyte/Thinkstock; p. 27 Jan Stromme/The Image Bank/Getty Images; p. 29 Steve Maslowski/Science Source/Getty Images.